This book belongs to

....

....

....

Text by Deborah Lock
Illustrations copyright © 2021 Helen Cann
This edition copyright © 2021 Lion Hudson IP Limited

The right of Helen Cann to be identified as the illustrator of this work has been asserted by her in accordance with the Copyright, Designs and Patents Act 1988.

All rights reserved. No part of this publication may be reproduced or transmitted in any form or by any means, electronic or mechanical, including photocopy, recording, or any information storage and retrieval system, without permission in writing from the publisher.

Published by
Lion Hudson Limited
Wilkinson House, Jordan Hill Business Park
Banbury Road, Oxford OX2 8DR, England
www.lionhudson.com

ISBN 978 0 7459 7833 8

First edition 2021

Acknowledgments
All unmarked scripture quotations are taken from the Holy Bible, New International Version Anglicised. Copyright © 1979, 1984, 2011 Biblica, formerly International Bible Society. Used by permission of Hodder & Stoughton Ltd, an Hachette UK company. All rights reserved. "NIV" is a registered trademark of Biblica. UK trademark number 1448790.

The scripture quotation on p.45 is taken from the International Children's Bible®, copyright ©1986, 1988, 1999, 2015 by Thomas Nelson. Used by permission.

A catalogue record for this book is available from the British Library

Printed and bound in China, November 2020, LH17.

Prayers *around the* World

DEBORAH LOCK
ILLUSTRATED BY HELEN CANN

LION
CHILDREN'S

The earth is the Lord's, and everything in it,
the world, and all who live in it.

Psalm 24

Contents

All the world, praise the Lord!	10
Sunrise in Southern India	12
Wheatfields of the Southern United States of America	14
Peaks of Peru	16
Hill and dale, United Kingdom	18
Blossom in Japan	20
Town and country, Germany	22
Gardens of China	24
Beaches on Pacific Islands	26
Coast of Norway	28
Harvest in Canada	30
Streets of Estonia	32
Thanksgiving in the United States of America	34
Days out in New Zealand	36
Land of ice and snow, Greenland	38
Plains of Kenya	40
Moonlight in Nepal	42
Praise the Lord from the Earth	44

All the world from East to West
Gives praise to you.
We lift our voices,
We clap our hands,
We stamp our feet,
 We dance, we sing,
We jump, we shout,
Give praise to you.

All the world from North to South
Gives praise to you.
All big things,
Mountains and lakes,
Waterfalls and volcanoes,
All small things,
Beetles and birds,
Seeds and flowers,
Give praise to you.

As the sun rises above tall peaks,
As awakening birds sing in the steamy jungle,
We take each new day with you.

Oh, the wonder of a new morning!
Oh, the warmth of the prairie breeze!
Oh, the sway of the ripening wheat!
Oh, the fullness of our daily bread!
Thank you for all that you provide
To fill our daily needs.

In the call of the condor,
Over the peaks of the Andes,
In the whistle of the wind,
Through the rush of the river,
In the warmth of the soil,
From the seed to a shoot,
Your care flows in everything,
And all grows strong and plentiful.

You give new birth, new blooms
You give joy within.
Over hill, over dale
You spread hope within.
With friends, with family
You shine love within.

From bustling cities
To shade of blossoming trees,
Lord, I seek your peace.

We thank you for our homes,
Help us to be kind to others.
We thank you for the countryside,
Help us to care for plants and animals.
Like seeds scattering in the breeze,
Help us to spread your love for all.

Sitting still, I look and listen.
You are everywhere: in my breath,
in the song of a nightingale,
in the ripple of the koi,

In the shape of a gingko leaf,
in the crafted arch of the bridge.

The breeze rustles the palm leaves.
The sea whispers inside a conch shell.
Of what wonders do they speak?
They speak of you and your creation.
How you know each of us,
just like every grain of sand.
How we are more special and unique to you
than the great variety of shells.
How your love for us is far greater
than our understanding.

North wind blows,
Seabirds swoop overhead.
Water laps over toes,
Fish wriggle beneath.
Clouds drift by,
Rain comes and goes.
Keep us safe in
your loving care.

Thank you for the harvest,
For all that you provide.
For sweet-tasting fruits from bush and tree,
in orchard, forest, farm and field.
May we share your riches with one another.

Church bells ring out, welcoming all,
Over the eaves where swallows nest.
Bicycle bells ring, trains toot, cars beep,
We go off to school through the busy streets.
Laughter rings out, it's time for fun,
Wrapped up warm, we kick the leaves.
Bless our homes, our work, and our play.

We come together for a time of thanksgiving.
We join together to support each other.
We meet together to share
what you have given us.
We celebrate together with thanks to you.
For our food, our freedom, and our country.

Through the beauty of the day
bring us joy and blessings.
Blue skies with fluffy white clouds,
Green forests and fields of grass,
Red rosy smiling faces,
Yellow rays of sunshine,
Pink petals, brown seeds,
Oranges and purple grapes,
Silver threads of spiders' webs,
Golden falling leaves,
Rainbows of sunlight through the rain,
Fiery sunsets and then black as night.

Long hours of daylight, then darkness reigns.
But in this land of ice and snow,
I am never alone.
You are with me, always.

Bwana, O Lord, shining light in the dark.
May peace be with us as we rest tonight.

The land yields its harvest;
God, our God, blesses us.

Psalm 67

From the rising of the sun
   to the place where it sets,
the name of the Lord
   is to be praised.

Psalm 113

Praise the Lord from the earth.
Praise him, you large sea animals
  and all the oceans.
Praise him, lightning and hail,
  snow and clouds,
  and stormy winds that obey him.
Praise him, mountains and all hills,
  fruit trees and all cedar trees.
Praise him, you wild animals and all cattle,
  small crawling animals and birds.
Praise him, you kings of the earth
  and all nations,
  princes and all rulers of the earth.
Praise him, you young men and women,
  old people and children.

Psalm 148